P9-AOA-433

THE MUD ACTOR

The
Mud Actor

CYRUS CASSELLS

Holt, Rinehart and Winston New York

Copyright © 1982 by Cyrus Cassells
All rights reserved, including the right to reproduce this
book or portions thereof in any form.
Published by Holt, Rinehart and Winston,
383 Madison Avenue, New York, New York 10017.
Published simultaneously in Canada by Holt, Rinehart and
Winston of Canada, Limited.

Library of Congress Cataloging in Publication Data
Cassells, Cyrus.
   The mud actor.
   I. Title.
PS3553.A7955M8   811'.54   81-13450   AACR2
ISBN Hardcover: 0-03-061371-X
ISBN Paperback: 0-03-061369-8

First Edition

Designer: Amy Hill
Printed in the United States of America
10 9 8 7 6 5 4 3 2 1

Some of these poems appeared in the following publications:
Sequoia, WPA.

The epigraph to the poem "Landscape with Traveler," by
Priest Saigyō, comes from *The Penguin Book of Japanese
Verse*, translated by Geoffrey Bownas and Anthony Thwaite
(The Penguin Poets, 1964). Copyright © 1964 by Geoffrey
Bownas and Anthony Thwaite. Reprinted by permission
of Penguin Books Ltd.

ISBN 0-03-061371-X HARDBOUND
ISBN 0-03-061369-8 PAPERBACK

FOR MY GRANDMOTHER ANNIE
FOR MY TEACHER CONCEPCIÓN JORBA
FOR GLENN WILLISTON
   "what the soul remembers is love"

THE NATIONAL POETRY SERIES

The National Poetry Series was established in 1978 to publish
five collections of poetry annually through five participating
publishers. The manuscripts are selected by five poets of national
reputation. Publication is funded by James A. Michener, Edward J.
Piszek, The Ford Foundation, The Witter Bynner Foundation, and the
five publishers—Doubleday, E. P. Dutton, Harper & Row, Random
House, and Holt, Rinehart and Winston.

THE NATIONAL POETRY SERIES—1982

Jonathan Aaron, *Second Sight* (Selected by Anthony Hecht)
Cyrus Cassells, *The Mud Actor* (Selected by Al Young)
Denis Johnson, *The Incognito Lounge* (Selected by Mark Strand)
Naomi Shihab Nye, *Hugging the Jukebox* (Selected by Josephine Miles)
Sherod Santos, *Accidental Weather* (Selected by Charles Wright)

⟍ ACKNOWLEDGMENTS

I would especially like to thank Carol Simone for her steady encouragement and support; Linda Gregerson, who took time to work with me at Stanford; and Glenn Williston, who helped me to "unearth" the world of Henri Lecroix, and whose intuitive gifts set me off on a mystical journey through fin de siècle France.

CONTENTS

1

ORIGINS

A CHILDHOOD

---

for my mother

Yes, your childhood, a fable for fountains now.
        —Jorge Guillén

1. THE WOMEN

My cotton shirts float on the line,
this one from India, those, from Africa, Guatemala—
And suddenly my grandmother appears,
in the South, in a straw hat, gathering
clothes before the rain,
while the clouds stall, the sun sinks
below a selvage of pine, and the dog days
unleash their soporific heat—
In the desert afternoon my mother stands, taking
the cottons from the line,
so I imagine them together, light-skinned, lyrical women,
each one describing
the same indelible motions—till I feel myself
through my mothers, my women selves
pausing among the sudden colors . . . a fluttering of
        sheets, shirts,
a childhood of breezes by the yard.

2. THE MAGIC CAT BONE

Grandaddy,
since your death I have been engaged

in rewriting
the family history:
When an English exiled Jew
married an African princess
all hell broke loose. . . .
If I could feel your laugh again—

Always you sit on the porch,
with your Don Quixote slimness and griot's gift
for charming a child;
even death can't stop
your storytelling:
I'm hearing Tar Baby, Br'er Rabbit again,
the woman who was slapped
by a ghost, and my favorite,
the magic cat bone:
"Boil a black cat," you say, "on the night
of the full moon, then slip the bones
gently through your lips;
the one that slides smoothest
is the magic bone. . . ."

Grandaddy, in the world I live in now
we say we have no need
of tales or talismans. But tell me,
can the magic cat bone
give me back the soul
I had as a child?
Yes, of course, you nod, waving the bone
like a wand.

And here I am again,
small, eternally

4

starting at strange sounds:
"Grandaddy, who's there?"

"*Haints* of slaves snowblind from the cotton."

3. DUENDE

for Concepción Jorba

Above the sill, the moon
is burning.
Softly, within the house, the bolero begins
with its deep magnetic sounds.
And I rise from my chair, driven
to dance—

I spread my arms and start to spin
around the room, alone.
As a child I danced like this—a dervish dancing
toward the ledge of God—
turning, turning before
my astonished family, never dizzying—
And now I seem to hear your voice,
as though you had said to me again
"Tienes duende":

Always I dance till the duende works
my body, suddenly aware of each small
death and birth of myself—while I spin,
miraculous as a blind man who senses
the moonlight brighten the brim of a well.

5

4. THE IMMANENT

Cicadas, the screened porch rife
with generations, the ceaseless
back and forth of the rockers, stiff and moon-white.
In my dreams the house is standing,
the porch, the apple trees still palpable;
Grandmother, I sit with you at the kitchen window,
singing, pressing the map of my palm
to the glass—

Last night I woke from a dream in which you said,
"You have grown so tall; I can kiss you
without bending"—and knew it had been years
since your death, years since I came
to the site of the house, and found
a sullen lot,
and went away—

But then the dreams began, returning
everything that had been razed:
the pines, the buried
house in which our bodies moved
—and still move, deep
in the summer.

THE MUD ACTOR

1. SICKNESS

Suddenly the body says night,
and it is sickness,
the thick dream I move through
like a mud actor.

Now stasis; I feel
the soft trees
november in my lungs.

And this is asthma:
I am that child
again, till dawn, exhausted in the slow
foraging for breath.

2. THE STALLED CHILD

As if I could forget the heat, the harsh light,
the land that would not yield a child
softness or color:
I look out over the parched flesh
of the Mojave, the place
I could never call home. Always
the primordial yawn of dry lakes.
The distant promise of water
—unreal. The crippled reach
of the joshua. I close my eyes

against the sun, the endless space,
and hear a small boy—stalled
and gasping:

Mud in my chest, no air;
I am drowning; I am going to die.

3.   REJUVENATION

As a child I felt old, the mud
clinging to my breath.
At twenty-two,
I sang to that child,
in the everyday havoc and joy,
carried him on my back—

And then I knew
we would have to grow young.

LA LUNA VERDE

for Lorca

Green, how I love you, green.
Green wind. Green branches.
Ship on the sea,
galloping horse on the mountain.
With the shadow on her waist,
she dreams by her railing,
green hair, green flesh . . .
         —Lorca, "Sleepwalking Ballad"

Suddenly the cante jondo chord of a guitar,
like wine spilling onto white cloth,
and your words, after so many years,
"Verde que te quiero verde,"
green, how I love you, green,
as in an open-air café, I feel myself
a student again, a young translator,
carrying my frayed copy
of *Romancero Gitano*, taking up the old quarrel
whether the moon is blue
or green.
Federico, at seventeen, I became possessed
by your voice in Andalucía, in Nueva York.
I loved you then
—as the chronicler of the gypsies,
as the visionary traveler
who mourned for Harlem.
You were my poet of blood and quicksilver,

of nard and moonlight—a sentient arrow
piercing me, as I tried to capture
the duende of your "Romance Sonámbulo"
—in the act of translation,
trying to make the leap
into your life,
which I make now, simply,
as the guitar exudes
a slow bloom of wine,
and I begin
to imagine your death:
I close my eyes and see
a tiny plaza, a summer moon poised
above a fountain,
and near that fountain,
a man who must be you,
rapt, focusing
on the splash of the water,
so as not to hear
the sound of shots from the hills
outside Víznar
—Víznar, which has become
another Calvary.
You hear a ticking
and look up:
A small boy is tracing circles
around you, dragging a gnarled stick
over the stones.
You take out your last cigarette,
watching him, and lift it
almost to your lips—then freeze
as he stops, drops the stick,
and takes from his pocket

a blood orange.
He opens his fruit
and sucks;
shyly, remembering his manners,
he extends his juice-stained hand
and offers you pungence.
And then he sees Death in your gaze
and runs down a narrow street.
A man in uniform appears
and touches your shoulder, and says,
"Señor, wake up.
It's time for your paseo."
And you go quietly.

Now the plaza is empty;
there is nothing but the moonlight
on the stones, the slow splash
of the fountain.

At wolf's hour, at the dark base
of a sierra,
the night is so beautiful: a few stars
over the vega,
cicadas, in the cistern
a water of tambourines.
I watch a man blindfold you
and think of de Icaza's words:
". . . nothing in life can equal
the agony of being blind
in Granada."
A chord resonates.
A breeze of Moorish ghosts
stirs the olive grove,

11

and I whisper in your terrified ear:
"Verde viento. Verdes ramas."
Green wind. Green branches.
Federico, I want to be your eyes,
I want to touch you
the way your voice touched mine
when I was younger,
the way a woman stands on a balcony
during the saeta, gripping the iron railing
in both hands, and sings
to the image of the crucified Christ.

At dawn there is no sun,
only the green moon—lucent and everlasting.
In its light,
I can see them clearly, the patent-leather men
who have no use for poetry.
They'd turn the vega
into a killing floor.
But as they pull the triggers,
they breathe the landscape
which *is* your poem:

Federico, I saw—
the flesh on their hands was green.

2

FIN DE SIÈCLE:
MEDITATIONS TO SATIE

GYMNOPÉDIES

for Glenn Williston

GYMNOPÉDIE # 1

The male figure recorded on a vase
       the ancient festivals of Sparta
the swirl
     of the discus
boys swaying
      like heliotropes to the sun
A piano music
      deft
and searching
      the white keys equivalent
to the plucking of lyres
      to the wheels of a carriage
turning
     through fin de siècle France
The picnic
     the cure of blossoms
has been postponed
      Imagine
a frail child tracing
      droplets of rain
on the carriage window
      dreaming of Greece
its salutary light
     "I will take you there"
said Jean-Yves
   "He gave me a vase and picture book of Greece"

15

GYMNOPÉDIE #2

A rocking horse bathed in light
                                    immobile
My childhood
                        the word *chrysanthemum*
on my tongue
                        How those flowers filled
my mother's vase
                            lit up my bedroom
Jean-Yves brought them
                                    It's been years
strophe
                    and antistrophe
sun
                    and shadow
I walk
                    to a familiar window
and start to play
                        the white sill
like a piano
                    When I stop
I close my eyes—
                        there is a balm
of ancient dancers—
                        I open my eyes
I'm alive
                    to stand in gold light
I loosen my necktie
                        I had choking fits
On days when health seemed
                                    as far away
as Greece
                    I sat in bed with my book

GYMNOPÉDIE #3

Jean-Yves

my father's friend

I was eighteen

when he took me to Greece

the age

of an ephebus

To press the keys

is to conjure a voyage

tablets for seasickness

a copy of *Salammbô*

return

through a music

liquid

reserved

like the deep

vowels of a well

We had reached

the Acropolis

its white ruins

calling us back

to Plato's time

In the distance

all Athens

the Aegean Sea

I felt

my poise

It was as if Jean-Yves

had shown me

in chrysanthemums

visions of Greece

the colors of health

In gratitude

I tried to speak
                              I turned
to him—

                       Jean-Yves
dead twenty years

                               Hear the clear and elegiac voice
of my piano—

                               Always silence chooses sound

        "I love you"

GNOSSIENNES

More sinuous
              than any other woman,
                            more sinuous . . .
You led me, at last,
to your room.
              As I remember,
there was a bouquet of Parma violets
on the chiffonier, you wore
a long-skirted, slender dress
from Brussels, a blue-gray muff
you stroked like a Siamese, finally
dropping it into my lap.

                     In the gaslight,
your angular face, cheekbones, the truculent rouge
that left its traces
on my fingertips;
touching your face, your throat,
I saw images—rising
as if from the bottom of a pond:
                     In another life, you were
a woman of Knossos,
dancing in ecstasy
in the olive grove,
grasping the swaying horns
of a bull, bearing libations
to the house of the double ax,
                    milk for the sacred serpent

19

that sleeps in the inner chamber, coiled
around a wand. . . .
                    You unraveled your chignon,
laying two opal-tipped pins
in my palm, as I said your name
under my breath: "Lucienne Victoire."
I searched your eyes
                    —like a small child trying desperately
to ferret your secret.

When did we begin to quarrel?
When you left the room, I pressed my face
to your muff.
                    More sinuous . . .

GNOSSIENNE #2

                    Anguish
then repose:
to leave off mystery and be lulled
between your breasts,
to watch through the iron grille
the sunlit maple—prodigal, shedding its leaves,
and on the lawn, the blue
shudder of a jay . . .
You imagined my beard
as a nest; my tongue darted out
to meet your nipple,
                    circling and foraging, circling
and foraging:
              "Little bird, little bird. . . ."

20

You were always in motion,
in pain.
But that morning scene
comes back to me,
simply: I have found
the lost scent of your quiet.

GNOSSIENNE #3

Undulant form:
                    a woman with the grace
of swans, who finally becomes blurred, transmuted
to a serpentine light
on water, a gold thread
                    at the surface . . .

            We were sitting in the Bois.
You kissed me and left me
your box from the milliner's to hold,
as I watched your figure moving
slowly,
            slowly down the promenade—the grave
rhythm of your skirt,
your hat with its spire
of soft plumage— And then
you disappeared into the street.

Sometimes I think I have built
a necropolis, a lie as fabulous
as the labyrinth of Minos:
Tell me your good flesh was real.

Tonight I feel your sad, accusatory eyes
on me again, as I begin
that letter I never sent:
"Ma femme . . ."

GNOSSIENNE: EPILOGUE

And yes, Léon told me, years later,
how they found your body
in a rue de la Mare pension,
with only a blanket
coiled round you, and on a table
not far from the bed,
a pitcher of milk,
a shredded violet . . .
Lucienne, why didn't you speak
of your illness,
instead of leaving me?—

In the dream of reunion,
I follow your gliding figure
like Ariadne's thread,
through the maze of the Edenic Bois,
past bicycles and parasols,
until you come to rest
beside the lake,
where you take out a pouch
and begin to toss
bits of bread, like coins
into the water
—as my soul splinters into fish
that dart to the surface
to receive your offering.

I call out to you.
In the time it takes for me to reach your side,
the lake freezes—children appear
on the ice; over there, the girl

in the gray ice-skating costume, she must be
the young Lucienne—and thaws.

"Mademoiselle Victoire, I believe
you left something," I say,
and give you the box
with the Greenaway hat.
You smile at me:
"Henri, how could I have forgotten?"
And I touch your arm—in relief.

It's such a sweet word, *forgiveness*.
Come, let me tell you the story
of a man and woman who failed
to comfort each other.

THREE PIECES IN THE FORM OF A PEAR

1

Actually, there are seven:
Four of the slices
were unannounced.

The first slice is a storm,
wind lashing the field, the baled wheat
scattered broadcast.

Douglàs comes down the hall with a candle.
A violent rain
strikes the casement.
Suddenly, we're frightened children again,
in fluttering nightshirts,
running from room to room:
"Renée, Maman, Papa,
there's rain on the parquetry,
and we can't shut the window!"—

"Douglàs, remember,
that night the Saône swelled,
and the house flooded.
We hauled buckets of water for days—
But let's forget all that. We need something
to keep our minds off of the storm."

Douglàs is in the mood for mischief:
"Henri, I've just the thing.
Let's get out Renée's ouija board."—

"O shades, O you who've crossed
to the other shore,
give us a message."

Is it wind—ethereal wind
that moves the planchette,
slowly spelling out:

HENRI LECROIX   DOUGLÀS BRIARTY
YOU ARE NOT ALONE

Thunder cracks.
Our eyes widen.
The cat stiffens
and broomsticks its tail—

And it's Douglàs, not the ouija,
who sneezes
                and blows out the candle.

2

Somewhere on the outskirts of Paris
a bird sings, perched
on the bar of our carriage.
We're one with the windmill's turn,
the horse's amble,
as we move through the streets,
a great menagerie,
where horns bleat,
a charwoman preens
into a puddle,

and two boys, two happy monkeys filch
tomatoes from a stand:
We didn't see; we've sealed our lips
to the shopkeeper.

It's so good to be back in Paris.
How could we forget?
We chose ourselves, chose
this charmed city
—unrivaled,
this city of shadows and mirth.

3

Franz is strolling in the garden:
Each rose is a Lied.
Eavesdropping,
hidden near the birdbath,
we follow the notes
like page turners.
We're about to surprise him
—our Polish friend
with the pure tone, who bears
more than a faint resemblance
to Charles Dickens.
He's so elegant, aristocratic:
The truth is
he's a motor mechanic;
at home,
he's a dandy,
with striped tie and walking stick,
a Maecenas of the flowers—

Wait, we've been discovered.
Franz descends upon us,
with his monocle:
"Well, what kind of flora have we here. . . ."

4

And I'm off to the rue des Martyrs
to visit my friend Marie,
a dancer who adorns herself
with snakes and feather boas.
I'm whistling a tenderness of cafés, a tune
I can't keep, a song
about absinthe, smoke, the endless foam
of petticoats,
as I spot her poster:

PRESENTING MADEMOISELLE DE FORTUNY
AND HER SERPENTINE PARTNER
MONSIEUR LALO

I find the tiny dressing room,
and there's Marie,
in her Grecian tunic
and gold headband, her mirrored face
rouged and floating
like a daymoon—
And the snake cage,
covered with an antique cloth
embroidered with red tulips.

I bring her dahlias.
"Of course you have no interest in me

as a woman," she smiles,
"only as a specimen
—a specimen for a writer."
She laughs her bell-clear laugh,
then takes her tablet,
her mysterious tablet—she says,
"A feminine thing, you know"—
and tells me her life
over tea: Today
it's her childhood in Bordeaux,
the affair with the zookeeper
that launched her career, more gossip
about "The Three Graces,"
Marie-Lalage, Marie-Celeste, and Marguerite,
"her bosom like a Spanish balcony"—

And when I return alone
to the rue de Parme, to my rented room
above the bakery,
I say, "Marie has nothing to be vain about,
really." But lately I notice
I've been thinking a lot
about a dancer whose dream
is to ride in the circus ring,
a dancer who has, shall we say,
certain acrobatic talents,
and putting literary interests aside . . .

5

"Faster, Henri, faster,"
Douglàs says,
"but watch out for those stones,

that rut in the road.
You'll spill the wine,
and we'll have nothing to drink
for our picnic."—

Lilac. Syringa.
Such a beautiful day
for a wheelbarrow ride,
a bit of nostalgia we indulge in
at the first blaze of spring,
as round and round the sunny Butte
we go careering
past a ragpicker, two laundresses
whispering in the shade,
and our friend Gérard
setting up his easel to record
the pointillist spread
of new leaves.

But suddenly, coming round a bend, oh God, we swerve
to avoid
a billy goat, smash into stone,
and Douglàs is hurled
over an embankment.

I call out to him—
                    No answer.
I climb down, splattered with wine,
and cull his body
from the vined slope,
drag him somehow to the wheelbarrow.
Then bedlam:

the barrow filling with blood; my heart beating
Please live, please live;
Gérard ripping his canvas
to close the wound; both of us
running, running;
the baying of a dog; the flap
of a startled chicken—
as a woman in a white apron
points the way:
"Over there, messieurs,
the house of Doctor Curtin."

6

Maurice, the little terrier,
places a solicitous paw
on the counterpane:
Douglàs is propped up on pillows, a vinegar cloth
wrapped around his head.
Our little group, "The Aerialists,"
have come to cheer him up.
Franz, out of character,
sings a bawdy song
to rival Aristide Bruant.
Claire-Yvette brings pansies and the cure
of her winsome smile.
Gérard gifts Douglàs
with a bottle of plum wine.
Now Franz switches to a lullaby,
and Vivienne, Armand, and Madame K.
provide a soothing chorus—

Later, when the group has left
for the café-concerts,
I sit beside Douglàs,
spooning him his favorite soup.
"Douglàs," I say, "imagine *me*
playing the nurse.
When we were boys
it was always you who brought
a chocolate in tinfoil,
or a marble,
to my bedside."

Douglàs manages a smile:
"Cousin Henri, at last
the tables are turned."

7

Douglàs is dozing under an oak,
still recovering, his felt hat
tipped over his face:
a study in lassitude.
Vivienne, with her straw hat and long dark braid
that divides her back, sits
at her easel;
now she turns and reveals
her opus, pointing at Douglàs
with her brush:
"Henri, see how that fly moves
over his hand; to the fly
his flesh is like a continent.

I'm painting it that way: just the hand
and the traveling fly."—

And with this seventh slice
called "Perambulations of a Fly,"
we conclude our pear,
not Cézanne perhaps,
but still appetizing.

NOCTURNES

NOCTURNE #1

The moon's great gasolier.
How many times have I felt it burn,
pure and lambent,
above my lifetime?
Moon of my childhood,
moon on the drowned faces in the Seine.

Tonight it illumines the soft fur
of a stray dog in the Bois, the white cleft
between a prostitute's breasts, the brass buttons
on the coat of a weary gendarme
—as if all Paris were one
floodlit garden of the moon.
A sleepwalking child, bathed in its glow,
pauses—
and sighs, and resumes
his calm pacing of the lawn,
while in another precinct, a young man snores
beside his bride, its veil on their thighs
an epithalamium of light. . . .

NOCTURNE #2

If I've chosen solitude
like a nun's cell,
let me forsake my vow,

now that the moon is cached
in black trees, in thin flags
of smoke: I am alone,
not a man, but a cat-quiet form,
motionless and frightened
in the opium-slow dark,
waiting to be released from each new
wave of pain.

There's a tapestry before me: a scene
of harvest home,
scythes, stars, and a moon
sewn above the sheaves,
the upraised arms of celebrants.
                                        I begin
to weep, moving my hands over it
like a blind man:
Henri-Martin, this can't be you.
A blackness like sand
in my eyes, a mound of it
against my heart;
where is the light?

But in the silence now
I seem to hear a voice:
"Henri, place your finger here."

And I reach up and find
the threads of the moon.

3

THE COLORS OF
ANOTHER HOME

TYPHOON

In shade, on cardboard squares, the sleeping obaasan,
wizened women in white kerchiefs resting
from their work, their tray left
in the hall before me, bowls cleaned
of green tea and rice,
while carp gleam in the pond,
like agile gold, like lamps—suspended
as if in the body of their dream.

I slide back the shoji panel
to see more clearly, lift
American eyes—a stranger measuring
a haiku of calm.

But already in the distance
the clouds appear,
like a flaw in a delicate
landscape screen.

It is the season of typhoon:
Above green terraces of rice, the sky
lowers—

And the wind lifts off
the roof of sleep.

> —Taki Ashina Yokosuka,
>   August 1978

THE CHILD YOU CALL EEYORE

for Kenzaburo Ōe and his fictional fathers

Your son tosses, sweet idiot wrapped
in sleep, in sweat.
You stand above him, *the father*, rumpled and phantom,
at zenith: In the dark he opens
his weak eyes, lifts
his small sleeves of fat. A shrill sob
shakes the room.
And you hold him, envelop him, the child
you call Eeyore, your brain-damaged child, your holocaust
of a firstborn.

What you live with: At first
you wanted him to die; you tried to flee, then chose
forbearance. Now, together, you form
a planet. You notice everything: his fear
of the toothbrush, his love of motion, how his face lights
on the subway train—
the bond, the conduit of pain between you
so supernatural, that when Eeyore burns
his hand on the stove, far away, in your office,
you feel the singe and cry
yourself: a man whose heart and senses
become a womb—

In wintry Tokyo, I find you,
two Eskimos, a fat
father and son,

trudging home at dusk from a full day
on the trains:
You say you would go down into the grave
with your child, as you brush thin snow
from his brow.

It is a tenderness beyond witness.

TO DREAM THE ENERGY OF CLAY

1

Let it be this life:
bell crickets, the pulse and process
of dusk, the soft breathing of bowls—cooling
in the shadowed yard, as the potter bends
above his wheel.
And always, beyond his farm, the gentle green
of tea bushes, terraces
of rice, the mountainside
where women sort the clays.

Let this be their lyric,
like veins of light:
Clay on our hands, in the hills our songs—our lives
so brief beside
the thousand years of the pine.

2

It is the autumn of flutes, imagine.
He stops his wheel: The sound of pines
swirls down from the mountain.

In the village, smoke lifts
from the kilns, the crone moon
rises, the clouds drift
white as cranes—

He holds up his gloves
of moonlight and clay.

3

Clear dawn: mountains and rivers without end.
A galaxy of reeds. The house,
pregnant with autumn. A thin gold
stains the shoji panels,
the shadows of approaching leaves;
all night the potter sensed
their trembling at the edge of sleep.

He wakes to his wife's good snore,
like cockcrow. Her breasts flow,
rife with daylight.

4

Know that in his garden
the shadows hold him like snow, everywhere
is balm.
What he knows of peace:
the pond, the perfect arch
of the bridge he wants to call
the floating bridge of dreams,
and the stalks of iris,
a slender quiet—

He remembers a gentleness:
In Sanzen-in, the world

was so still. He paused
on a veranda, his eyes closed—his lids
suddenly a deep green.
It was reunion, or the end
of desire.
All voices stopped. The water stilled
over the sculpted stone.

And for one moment he felt
the soul of the garden—released,
and knew he contained it,
mute and clean
as a vessel of clay.

5

In his sleep,
the panorama of seventy autumns.
Clay spinning for decades.
The chant of the dragon kiln:
Cobalt
　　　Alumina
　　　　　Rhythm of fire,

as he takes a piece of his flesh
like a wine-bright leaf,
and presses it into the clay.

It is his own blood he pours
over the bowls, like kaki, the red
persimmon glaze.

The dream is a kiln:
Flames of wild grass
engulf him—

He wakes with reed-patterns
on his heart.

6

Let it be this life:
dreams, the mystery of tea things, the village
salted in time.

Dried persimmons and a stilled wave
of earth:
a vase assembling
in a shaft of sunlight.

7

And he takes from the bamboo shelf
a bowl with the feel
of mountains in it, recalling
the stillness and musk
of Nara, where deer lick
human hands.
This clay is almost flesh.
How could he ever live
without these shapes of love and use?

LANDSCAPE WITH TRAVELER

At a roadside
Where a clear stream bubbles
In the shade of the willows,
"Just for a while," I said,
And still have not gone.
            —Saigyō

In Japan, I seemed to have stopped
in the middle of a road.
And why should I stop here—except to pause
and be painted in, to feel my life
a fragment of this landscape.

Centuries of rice, the green
syllables of the mountain.
At the height of summer, amid the flames
of reeds, a stillness
as of snow piled
in a silver bowl: This is the stillness
at the core of breath.
As the cranes lift, I feel
no moment—

Toward horizons, sea-breath, toward a mountain that fell
from the sky, the Buddhist pilgrims
are traveling; their prayers seed
this island of shrines—

The day speaks, returns me
to myself:

Here is the created road.
Go farther.

THE PILLOW

He touches her breasts, a sunburned neck, a back bent
from years in the fields.
And now she lifts to him in the moonlight
her belly, as pale
as a Nō mask—

It has been like this
for decades, the two of them
lying together on the futon:
See, their bodies have twisted
into an old branch.

RUMORS

1. THE POND

Among reeds, lotus, the breath of still flowers, her face
floats. Tabi like snow, a tight-wound, orange-colored
obi, the rich red flash
of her kimono
color the pond:
a picture of a woman
waiting.

A man enters the frame, stands
beside her. She can almost feel
his touch, so familiar, though they are still
separate:

It is a dream. A panel moves: Her husband peers,
old, predictable—
She starts and drops a stone, disturbs
the surface of that mirror.

2. THE FLOATING WORLD

When the snow fell, he was in
another province. She would not release
the bond. She lay in bed and felt
a shiver of cold, a pine needle—
until her breasts were buried under
a fan of needles.

At dusk she woke and found
her body, fisted and hollow
as a conch. She drifted, passed
through the panels:
In another room women were gathered
around the brazier, whispering, warming
their hands—their skin, their tiny palms, suddenly
transparent, as slowly she shifted
her gaze—

How simply she had left
the floating world, that fragile house
of wood and paper.

BOUND FEET

---

for Winston Tong

There was a woman of Ming snow.
In the name of love,
her feet were bound—so that a man might touch
the tiny shoes, and whisper
Lotus, lotus. . . . Her pained face flickered
on the surface of tea.
Behind her phoenix screen, the secret
cached in white cloth:
blood, crushed bone.

At festivals the women gathered, hobbling together,
a forest of canes—their bodies
the attitudes of willows—

For a thousand years, the women
were crippled into deer. In the name of love,
their souls froze into jade.

THE SERVANT (MUSIC AND BLINDNESS)

after Tanizaki's *A Portrait of Shunkin*

Enlightenment comes,
They say,
Like a knife in the inner ear . . .
Like lilacs crashing
Through snow.
      —Rose Anna Higashi: "Satori"

Music and blindness, the ache
of pure allegiance, two kotos
blending in the dead of night, a song
as quiet as lust.
Shunkin, I speak to you in the silence
after the locusts' trill, the last chord
of your samisen, the lark you called
"Drum of Heaven."
Under the pines, the resinous moon, the stone
bears this inscription:

          NUKUI SASUKE
      Servant of Mozuya Shunkin

Even in death I kneel—

At first I was no more than a hand
to you, your father's shopboy
guiding you

to your music lesson.
In secret, I would close my eyes
and pluck your samisen,
imagining your world
of black snow—
Then one night, after many years,
you called me to your room:
A pomegranate burned the white lake
of your belly; you laughed,
then took it away, saying,
"Do anything you want
with my body."
I opened the fruit and trickled the seeds
between your breasts.
Red sparks, splinters of coolness—
I pressed wet jade
to your eyes, tongued your lids, wanting
to give you sight.
Telling you spring I became spring:
You were my lover; I pierced you
with color—orange, vermilion, plum.
I whispered *Moonlight pooled*
in the hollow of your throat;
in the night, your breasts, your thighs
somehow silver—

Shunkin, a generation passes
in the space of a dream—our four children
you gave away at birth.
In the hush after the last child,
you held my Shino teacup
to your breast, releasing
a ribbon of milk—as if it could end my thirst
for a son.

Forgive me, I was the intruder
who slashed your koto's strings, who lifted the kettle
to scald your face, as a flock of geese
splintered in the sky—their cries
muted by ours. . . .
From the maid's room I stole
a sewing needle. Then I sat before a mirror,
very still. A calm light
fell over my face.
And then it was your face
I saw, your throat of snow
—scorched by my own hand. The needle
glittered between my fingertips—I had to give you back
your beauty—I drove it into my eyes. My lenses
shattered. I listened:
I heard the thunder of lilacs
crashing through snow.
My head blazed. I groped
through the hall—the wounds unraveling
everything of autumn.
In the flood of the full moon
I found your breathing;
I came to you again, a servant, jubilant
in blindness.

STOIC POSE

for David Politzer

1. THE LESSON

At dawn, they splashed his cheeks with cold saké.
Then they led him to a room—brusquely
sliding back the panels—
where a man's, a peasant's body
lay on the mat, naked
except for stripes of shadow
across the flesh:
This was his introduction
to death.
They positioned him near the corpse, saying:
The boy is samurai;
he must learn.
In his hands they placed
the heavy sword,
as quietly he began to cry. . . .

Later, they hung his small, blood-flecked kimono
on a bamboo pole:

He was five when they taught him
to quarter the bodies.

2. MANHOOD

And then the elders said:
You are a man now, a samurai. You will be asked
to endure anything.
How could they tell him
he would take the head
of his beloved friend, as second
in the ritual suicide:

At the appointed hour,
he raised his sword;
for him, there was only Kyūnosuké
in his white robes
falling forever,
and the words of the Zen priest
Yōgetsu:
Strive for mastery. Live as though your body
were already dead.

3. THE BEGGAR

One day an old beggar stopped him on the road—his plea
like the drone of a mosquito.
It happened so quickly:
When the old man lifted his empty bowl,
he severed his head.
But what he saw in the wizened face
haunted him for years:
not a look of terror,
but of beatific love.

4. SINKING STONE

At his lord's command,
he brought the child before him.
It was understood
that the ancient enmities
would be forgotten, and the child
would be spared.
But a samurai appeared,
carrying on a tray
the skulls of the enemy clan,
lacquered in vermilion,
as his master called
for the boy's tiny skull:

It was the spray of blood across heaven—

That night, beyond the whorl
of the raked courtyard,
in Yōgetsu's garden,
he came upon a pool
which cupped the moon,
and pressed his scarred face
into the water,
and craved to become sinking stone.

5. STOIC POSE

They branded his woman before his eyes,
and what he kept, days later,
was the smell of tatami

and seared flesh, a flurry of snow
outside the teahouse of the inn
where he felt her agony.
He could not flinch:
A samurai, he saw his master wound
the round-faced maid,
O-en,

and could do nothing.

6. ZEN PAINTING, FIFTEENTH CENTURY:
ASCENDING SOUL

When he opened his belly,
his heart cradling
O-en's shame,
it was autumn in the universe.
Clear leaves fell around him,
as Yōgetsu, with his keening brush,
saw his soul separate
into a thousand fireflies,
of which the priest-painter captured four
and pressed them into his scroll.

THE BLOSSOMS

for Yasunari Kawabata

It is always a war. Masahiko went off to die. Before he left, he sloshed the tea on Kyoko's sleeve. She went with him to the station. She did not say, "Kamikaze, you will die, and the boy will be mine, only mine." He held her; she felt his blind cheek brushing hers. Then simply, she lifted the kimono sleeve, and waved, as his train started:

This is how he will remember me. No tears. Only this stillness, this cold knowledge opening inside me— like a paper flower dropped into a pond.

*

When the news came, the boy lay asleep on a mat. She went out into the garden and let the blossoms flood her lap.

THE WOMAN WITH THE TANGLED HAIR

for Yosano Akiko

At twilight Tekkan stands by the door. Your name, "Tomiko," falls like a leaf. I sit in the faint light, before the mirror, watching the liquid white of my eye, pretending not to hear. He lifts his hand toward the dark garden, as though you were still standing beneath the plum.

And then he goes out under the pear trees, where the shadows are thicker than blood.

If I sit at the mirror and say your name now, as he does, it's because, in this cold hush, the sound of it is clean.

I get up, go out to the yard. In the moonlight I find Tekkan lying in the grass. A thin line of ants darkens his cheek. I brush the ants away, and hold him.

All the time I feel you in the breeze, in the clear night sky.

Tomiko, sister, stay back. What can I say to make you let him go? I have only this tangled hair—against your ghost.

THE COLORS OF ANOTHER HOME

In the charged moment when the scarecrow raised
his shimmering arms, tossing the crows
into violent light,
a voice said clearly:
Sink deeper into the world.
The reeds swayed. I felt
the flesh of my palm tingle,
heard the crunch of gravel
under my sandal,
like the cracking of pond ice,
as slowly the very landscape echoed
and became familiar:
This is called déjà vu—

Then I saw myself
under the regression
a woman bending over a pond
in the fifteenth century, a feudal lord
drowning in a boat:

And my soul whispered
I am Japanese
—these mountain blues, these mute, cool greens
the colors of another home.

THE MEMORY OF HIROSHIMA

for the survivors and for myself

The people of Hiroshima ask nothing of the world
except that we be allowed to offer ourselves as an
exhibit for peace.
> —Shinzo Hamai, Mayor of Hiroshima, 1949

We believed we would be safe in Hiroshima.
We boarded the train
with our burden of rice cakes
and rolled mats, toys, swaddling clothes,
and cardboard luggage
tied with string.
We were a family
of four children, fleeing
starvation, the endless lists
of the war dead,
forced to leave behind
our widowed mother,
and ailing grandmother;
we were entrusted with an uncle
who lived secure
in Hiroshima.
It was the hope
of hegira—
three days of hard travel
to a kinder life—
the winged words
of a Nō play:

"We go, our hearts unhindered
as the flight of clouds. . . ."

In time, there was only
the slow ribbon of our journey
unwinding under the sky,
the dull rocking of the cars,
the windows scrolls of green,
as the trains steamed
through planets of rice, the land
dotted with pillboxes.
Always I sat in stiff seats, facing
my older sister, Michiko,
caged in her dark, proper traveling dress,
so wrong for Japanese summer,
the baby, Taiji, lively in her arms,
her thin, inquisitive brows
the black-winged traces
of my sumi brush
—while Isamu, in his schoolboy's cap,
drummed his knees to a fine tattoo,
or tapped the window.
To calm him,
I took from a box
the gold-braided German marionette
my grandfather gave me
as a boy,
and recited strands
of a puppet play,
—a beautiful michiyuki passage.
In the moment of performance,
working the strings,
I felt the warm, ingenuous gaze

of an old couple,
two passengers across the aisle,
and craved
invisibility, the black, anonymous clothes
of a puppeteer's apprentice,
that could free me to be,
not Yoshi Nakamura,
but the shadow of a doll,
masterful and hidden
from death,
hidden, at seventeen,
from the carmine paper
of a draft notice,
from the terrible pledge
Yes, I would die,
I would die for the emperor.
I closed my eyes and recovered,
in one long breath,
Doolittle's raid:
the panic of parasols,
the crush of running bodies
against the lunch stand,
bowls of seaweed soup splattering
onto the counter,
as my brother, Mamoru, was knocked
from the wooden stool—
my last glimpse of him
a ripped sleeve, a small window
filled with flesh,
that simply vanished.
I opened my eyes,
put the puppet away, remembering
our fruitless search,

as an earlier maze
of Tokyo streets meshed
with a world of aisles and strange depots,
as a needle of trains
threaded a weariness
from station to station:
Isamu vomiting on the platform;
the sting of the baby's cry;
the haggard mask of my face
in the glass,
stars, leaves, clear landscapes
flowing through it,
and the image of my mother
in shadow, at the family shrine,
wiping the photographs of the dead—

On the last night,
there was a note of moonlight
pinned to our seats,
its white message finally
passing over our faces—
the moon itself,
a dropped camellia,
a strange and distant bloom,
as I watched
my sister's sleeping form, noting
the black thick-heeled shoes
that hurt her so,
and in her moonlit lap,
the rhododendron flower
picked near Kyōto.
After the black music of ruined cities,
Tokyo, Ōsaka, Kōbe,

we found Hiroshima at dawn,
on the morning of the fourth,
beautiful, intact,
the river Tenma tinged
with gold and pomegranate.
We walked from Yokogawa station
till the sky paled,
following the meanders of the river
to the house
near Sumiyoshi bridge,
where we found the poignant eyes
of Noboru,
who did his best to hide
his bad limp
under his yukata.
To our surprise,
he had another guest
as well, a young postal clerk,
Shinkichi, who added to
the noisy and jubilant reunion:
tears of saké
dribbling onto a sleeve,
the skin around our eyes deepened
to a plum blush.

On the second day,
Michiko stepped out for fish,
the blue fabric of the morning—pierced
by a siren.
At the all-clear, we men roused
for tea and talk,
the gentle swaying of fans
over the low table.

There was a lacquered screen
beside me, the carved arc
of a maple:
In Japan, always
the delicate, deciduous branch,
the gentle sadness
of autumn in the soul,
even in summer.
The panel was open; I could see
a stone lantern,
a swatch of shade tree.
In the kitchen, on a cutting block,
were the shards
of a blue teacup, splinters
of vermilion reeds:
my morning clumsiness, my habit
of pressing the warm teacup
to my cheek,
whenever I was lost
in thought.
I had just wiped
the stained hem of my yukata.
Isamu was playing in the yard.
The baby was asleep
in the next room.
We were talking about
work, the politics of the war,
when I veered away,
imagining out loud
a lazy escape
under the shade tree.
The impact came
at the moment of soft laughter.

There was a shock of light.
The house shredded.
The impression of the day,
which was the hushed wedding
of white and gold,
of summer light brushed
on paper panels,
became black and crushed.
I did not know
what to do:
I no longer seemed to have
a body,
only a feeling of searching
through cruel heat and ash.
In my mind's eye, I tried to lift
the baby, Taiji,
and then, suddenly, I realized
we were dead.
I hovered near the wreckage,
in shock. It looked as if
someone had taken
the silver flat of an iron
and pressed it into the city.
Then, gradually,
I felt myself rising toward
a great and welcoming light.

                *

Now, coming out of a mountain tunnel,
I shield my eyes from the sudden explosion
of sunlight, catching
the brief rumor of my face
in the glass,

and know that I am Cyrus Cassells,
riding on a train
to Hiroshima,
clasping a memory
no one can explain away,
rippling back and forth
between worlds,
as if all time
were the surface of a single pond,
as if the soul
were a radio, and each station
a life, an incarnation,
which could be yielded
by the turning of a mental dial,
the mind of a young traveler
turned to give you
Yoshi Nakamura
in World War II Japan.
I think of death and beyond,
how I learned
that Mamoru did not die,
but was sheltered
by a candymaker and his wife,
then enticed
to live as their adopted son
—a wartime tale
of enchantment;
how I saw our mother Omie
alone, dispossessed, taken in at last
by her in-laws,
only to die one winter
shortly after the war.
And what is one family's death

on the killing floor of history?
Not the panoply of war,
the terms of conflict,
what the soul remembers
is love:
a search through the snow of ash and ruined flesh
for my lost Michiko, Isamu, Taiji,
a search through a thousand streets of Tokyo
for Mamoru—
I look from the train
—towns, fields gliding by me
on my pilgrimage,
and feel
a perfection, an order, a brotherhood so literal
it dazes me, for truly
we are each other,
and if our legacy
is obscenity, ceaseless war,
and war a fathomless falling away
from consciousness,
then this is the nightmare
we all wake from;
let us wake out of the nightmare—annealed.

We who have the duty to refuse
to kill, we who have the genius, the power,
to darn our world,
we who are both human and divine,
if we could stand together at last, in the place
where the victim and murderer embrace,
where there is no enemy, no evil,
no guilt nor judgment,
only ourselves

and this juggernaut of fear;
if we could stand,
and you could take from me
the memory of Hiroshima,
as a bit of burden
to cup in your hands, a share of ash
to scatter in gentle wind
as a talisman against all war,
for whoever holds the memory of Hiroshima
there is no choice
but peace.

I believe I died
to know the lust for peace,
to know fully and forever
the sacredness of life cannot be sacrificed
for any end.
And I want to tell you
how in the museum
I had to stop myself from crying out
at the photographs of Hiroshima
that matched my lucid dreams and recall,
how I looked at the singed
and terribly wounded hibakusha
without recoil, swabbing them with my eyes, my love,
because I recognized and claimed at last
my own experience—
these are my people
also, this is what we chose
for ourselves, for you,
and for the world to remember,
as unconsciously we chose to die
in protest, trying to say

the quality of life is more important
than survival—
how I learned that the soul can cradle
so much suffering, so much horror,
and still remain whole.

Last night, in the youth hostel, I dreamed again
the hell screen of the bombing:
A blinding flash.
A brutal shattering of the panes.
Again, women and children dressed in flames,
a human smoke.
Everywhere the charred weeping of blood,
the damaged wrappers of skin.
The country of ash. The country of ash.
Today, in the August sun, I walk,
one week after the anniversary,
with my friends, Atsushi and Takayoshi,
always seeing against the sky
the raw, obstinate, cracked-shell statement
of the Atomic Dome.
And what can I say
in the Hiroshima jazz club
to the young Japanese, who,
searching my eyes for American guilt,
asks me, "Cyrus, do you feel shame in Hiroshima?":
"No, can you understand,
I believe I died *here*?"—

I had to retrace my steps;
I had to make myself walk
through the sound of my own
weeping for the world,

to crawl again, from memory,
across the charred, keening floor
of Hiroshima,
the thick dream I moved through
like a mud actor,
a blight of rooftiles, splintered wood,
fumes and searing heat,
through the ragged breathing and the netted sounds
of the dying,
which are indistinguishable
from those of the newborn,
to crawl through the bald epiphany of the words
I am still alive,
beyond the useless tatters
of my own flesh,
and the map of trauma
—which has vanished now,
amid river sounds, a noisy relief
of children.
I had to return, once again,
as a visitor,
because I believe
not one consciousness was destroyed
in Hiroshima.
I had to hear
the purposeful ring of the peace bell,
to see the bronze figure
of the young radiation victim,
Sadako Sakichi,
with her arms uplifted and gently weighted
with the many paper cranes
that are Japanese blessings.
I had to find and embrace

the deep form and unity of the world.
It is the new flesh, the sun's cleansing, the crane's flight
flecked with remembered ash.
It is the heartbeat
of a reconstructed city, a slow walk
through Hiroshima, the sound of a radio
turning on. Everything in life
is resurrection.

   —Hiroshima to San Francisco,
    1978–1981

 POSTSCRIPT

The Mud Actor was conceived—intuitively—as a single work, with the three sections written simultaneously to create a poetic triptych, a book of identities that ultimately embraces the possibility of reincarnation.

For my part, the poems represent a period in my life when I experienced what some call "reincarnational bleedthroughs" as well as other psychic phenomena—a period of intense psychic upsurge and new perception, which culminated in my journey to Japan. I had no previous framework for these experiences, and in my urge to communicate, poetry became my favored tool.

My working methods included meditation as well as other states of altered awareness, and the use of a technique called "hypersentience" or "hypnotic regression"; this is a simple and straightforward process involving relaxation of the mind and body that allows the subconscious material to come to the fore and enables the subject to move backward to any point in time, even into a "past life," while the conscious mind is "at rest." This was done alone, and under the guidance of others.

77

This technique is less mysterious than it sounds. Many artists work in a state of light trance without ever being aware of it. They are not aware of this trance because the mediumistic impulse, the actor's impulse, and the powers of the mind in general have been so misunderstood in our culture. The flexibility of consciousness is feared, or simply ignored.

This book was a constant process of self-revelation. I was working with the puzzle of my own personality here, moving through the annealing voices of my fictional and past-life personae to explore the mystery of my individuality, and often I was as much psychic detective as poet. I was learning to trust my mind in a new way. This was sometimes a strain, for often I found myself dealing with material I had little or no conscious knowledge of at all—which necessitated many trips to libraries and other sources of information. In my research, and in the refining process of the poetry, I tried to remain faithful to these visions or memories, to embroider as little as possible.

The section "Fin de Siècle" began when I asked myself why Satie's "Gymnopédies" felt so personal, so important to me. I found, to my amazement, that by meditating on Satie's work I received vivid impressions of fin de siècle France, and so, for several months I stepped into the world of Henri Lecroix almost daily through my musical meditations. I experienced these poems in a rich, hallucinatory way—with a deep immersion. This was especially true in the case of the epilogue to the "Gnossiennes" where the drama of reunion seemed enacted as if for my benefit, as if I were simply the witness, the amanuensis.

"The Memory of Hiroshima" was simply at first a

scene of a conversation—violently bleached, then burned away—like a frame of film jammed in a projector that finally incinerates the image—a scene played, again and again, in sleep, from earliest childhood. And then, in late July of 1978, at my host family's home outside Tokyo, the nightmare became lucid: My dream world became a vast crematorium, a panoramic hell screen, which often shocked me awake, screaming. In my special pilgrimage to Japan, I had been prepared for almost anything but this. It seemed clear that I had died in a bombing during the last world war, and gradually, a series of coincidences and illuminations led me to Hiroshima. In that city, one week after the anniversary of the blast, I decided my experience needed to be told. Drawings of the nuclear devastation made by the hibakusha, the victims of Hiroshima and Nagasaki, have been collected in the book *Unforgettable Fire*; as a "psychic hibakusha," I needed to draw my own picture—with words, as each of us is, in turn, charged to bear witness.

So much in our culture is silenced, buried out of fear, and I was unable to speak of my experience for some time. I would like to thank the people who listened to me when I felt ready, especially Glenn Williston and Ann Hinkel, who helped me with the difficult process of reconstruction and release, and with the verification process currently underway in Japan.

For a long time I resisted this memory. I was simply afraid—afraid I would be turned to salt or stone if I culled it. But then I realized that only by examining and reliving the memory of Hiroshima could I be truly released from it. In all the mnemonic experiments that went on behind this book, none of the work was undertaken out of idle curiosity, but in a spirit of purgation and enhancement of my present life. It is my belief that most of us live, unconsciously, under the burden of a traumatic past, and so memory and the act of remembering become important tools in our eventual release and progression in life.

One day, when I was seventeen, a voice inside me said, "The title of your first book of poems is *The Mud Actor*." Who, what is "the mud actor"? I wondered. I immediately associated it with my childhood asthma; hence, the title poem. But in reconstructing the memory of Hiroshima, the mud actor came to mind once again: I found myself, as Yoshi Nakamura, focused on the charred ground of Hiroshima; I felt myself trapped and trying to move through a thick, ashen darkness. The house, my body, my loved ones, the world as I had perceived it only a moment before had been decimated; there was simply, suddenly, nothing. Then, very slowly, out of the confusion, I recognized the flicker of my own consciousness. Recalling this scene was perhaps the most painful moment of my life, and yet, it was only then that I understood with all my being the continuity of life. This is the mud actor; this is where my book was born.

I can no longer accept a world view that offers no hope, that denies all evidence of spiritual heritage or survival. As a poet, I can't offer any more or less than rumors of our own indestructible beauty. We have to find and touch our indestructible selves, to fight the illusion of powerlessness, of final negation. We who have the genius, the power, to darn our world. We who are both human and divine.

—Cyrus Cassells

 NOTES

1. ORIGINS

Haints—ghosts (dialect)

Duende—a word the Andalusians use to describe the almost demonic possession of an artist (often a performer), or anyone, in the act of creation. Anything done with a peculiar intensity or passion is said to be done with duende.

La Luna Verde—On August 19, 1936, the poet Federico García Lorca was taken to an olive grove outside Víznar, and shot, and buried in an unmarked grave.

2. FIN DE SIÈCLE: MEDITATIONS TO SATIE

This section is part of a musical-poetry performance piece that evolved over months of work with the Satie recordings of the pianist Aldo Ciccolini; the poems are lyrics in

83

the root sense of the word, and were written primarily to be recited to the music.

Gymnopédies—a word Satie coined himself, probably derived from the Gymnopaidiai, the ancient summer festival for Spartan men and boys.

Gnossiennes—another Satie-ism that suggests "woman of Knossos," the ancient city of Crete.

Gnossienne: Epilogue—This poem corresponds to the music of Satie's "Gnossienne #5."

Three Pieces in the Form of a Pear—The title is a characteristic Satie joke, a response to his best friend Claude Debussy, who had criticized his work for being "formless."

3.   THE COLORS OF ANOTHER HOME

The Woman with the Tangled Hair—a name given to the famous Japanese love-poet Yosano Akiko (1878-1942) by her husband, the poet Tekkan, after the title of her classic first book, *Tangled Hair*. The poem centers on the famous literary love triangle between the two poets and the poet Tomiko Yamakawa, Akiko's best friend.

Michiyuki—the "journey" passage of a bunraku puppet play that usually ends in the "love-death" of the puppet protagonists.